June, Oct 98

Love & Light.

The
Omano Oracle

Jack S

Cover Art by Isabelle Rudolphi

Medicine Bear Publishing Co.
P.O. Box 263
Taos, N.M. 87571

ISBN#0-9651546-8-8

Library of Congress CCN# 97-070856

Dedication

This book is dedicated to Gillian.
Her love, devotion, and encouragement have made these words possible. And to all Earth's Turning Children of Light who fearlessly cross the threshold of their heart to ascend the stairway to their shining star.

William Wordsworth, the great poet, has said that poetry is:
"Emotion recalled in tranquillity."

Perhaps in these writings the reverse may also be true. In the turmoil of our lives, within the deepest emotional experiences, the words of a verse may awaken a deep memory within our heart; a recollection of a timeless light realm where soul did once dwell. If, even for the briefest moment, that memory stirs...you have returned home.

Hold this book close

to your heart

so that your essence

and the essence of the book

become one.

Open the Oracle

at any page,

may the guidance you seek

unfold before you.

A guide from the stars

to lighten your journey

A guide from the stars to

remember your way home

A guide from the stars to

help you remember who your are

Introduction

Is there a name we can call you?

*What label can you place upon the starry night
to call the stars, the planets closer to you?
What name would you use?
What voice resplendent in its own glory, its sound?
The name, the sounds are not the link for I come to you on
beams of light and love so you may see the radiance that lights
your soul on its eternal path, winding its way through a myriad
of stars. The sound is but an echo of a distant past, for light is
now the vehicle returning to the source to be once more
reflected upon the earth. The journey starts once again.*

*I will tell of light and thought. Thought is of a much higher
vibration and will travel in your time scale accelerated by the
force of light. To see the two as apart is not the right way, for
light is the driving force behind thought. I speak of thought
but not thinking there is a great difference between the two.
The greatest force in the universe is a single thought powered
by light, for this is how our worlds were created.
Let, therefore, your thoughts be driven by the light of awareness.
In understanding this simple truth, you will transform
darkness into light.*

Ask not the meaning of love but perceive how its magic changes the mundane to the magnificent...The ordinary to the extraordinary and the long nocturnal vigil into a golden dawn.

Heal with love and light...they are far more effective cures than any earthly elixir from your drug store.

Death is also the birth of all that expresses beauty and reality. Without death there can be no dignity, no grace, no life.

Listen to the silence between each note when love plays her enchanting melody on the golden strings of your heart, magically melting your mind with the magic of her music.

PART I

The Oracles

*We greet you
in the silent space of your heart,
with words, not to influence your mind,
that is not our purpose.
These words are sent
with golden arrows of light
to pierce your heart.
Read them with love
and you will surely feel our presence.*

Each day is a new beginning,
an opportunity to experience
the very depths of life.
Each moment is a doorway
to the timeless realm of reality.
Sands of time may trickle slowly
through the measured hour glass of mind,
but mind is only your traveling companion.
In Truth, you are much more.
When the silence of a moment descends,
you can glimpse
the eternal being you truly are;
a spark of the divine essence,
revealing itself as love.

*Many may believe in a gradual process of
ascension, but we say in truth...
each moment a heart opens in love, soul's
frequencies reach the highest pinnacle.
To share this love with many
is life's true purpose.*

Remember always,
wisdom communicated by the power of love
is multiplied many times.
Share the love you find within your heart
and use the wisdom of your words,
enabling those you touch
to perceive their own inner values.
When words have fulfilled their purpose,
then it may be possible to touch deeper levels.
This is true communication;
blending the wisdom you have acquired
with your mind,
with the love you find in your heart.

Life is a journey into the unknown,
a journey to be traversed with trust.
Whilst you can never acquire a map,
there are nevertheless,
many signposts upon the way
guiding you safely towards your destination.
Your journey requires
no distance to be traveled,
only a pilgrimage towards
your own heart center.
On your inner route there may be many fears
and memories of past experiences,
attempting to deter you
from your quest for Truth,
but these will surely fade
when the beam of awareness,
shines forth brightly on your path.

Love is like the spreading root of a great tree,
stretching deep into the earth.
To find the depths of love's root,
you may have to dig deeply
into the soil of your being.
Perhaps you rested for a while
in the leafy shade
waiting for fruits to appear in their season,
but were there not tears within your eyes
as time passed and you were left hungry?
In Truth, love's fruit has no season,
it is there at all times.
Discover its roots deep within
and you will surely celebrate
the golden harvest of love with many souls
so eager to share the nectar of your fruit.

*Do you not remember
the regal dwelling of light
your spirit left so long ago?
It is from that silent space we touch.
We can surely rejoice now in the love we share
with so many brothers and sisters of light.
When you remember,
they too may recall that ancient time
when they shared the blessings of our kingdom.
But there is no crown
to be placed upon your head
for we all truly share the very same throne
in our eternal palace of light.*

*All that glistens is not gold
Nor can reflections stored in the memory
bring new light.
We do not say past memories have no value,
but see how they can form dark clouds
over your sun.
Climb to a vantage point
at the peak of your being
and watch the clouds magically dissolve
into the ever flowing water of life's river.
You may see this as a cleansing process,
but in truth it is only clear observation,
without judgment.
In this golden space your true light will glisten
with ever renewing splendour.*

The plaintive cry
of an injured child may be heard
as you move close
to the deep well of the unconscious.
Perhaps when you gaze into the depths
there may seem to be many
forbidding fears to face
before a rescue attempt can be made.
But the depths must be penetrated
with great courage, enabling the inner child
to experience the gift of light
awaiting in the fresh fertile fields of your being.
How deeply she longs to dance
among the flowers and trees
and to join the songbirds greeting a new dawn.
Remember always, she is your child,
a part of yourself that you may have forgotten,
but now awaits your reclamation.
Take her hand
and celebrate life's dance together.

There are no answers to reveal love's mystery,
love cannot be understood by your mind,
only lived and experienced by your heart.
In moments of silence, when mind is absent,
love gracefully enters
the space you have prepared.
Spaces in your life
are fertile soil for love to germinate;
look not to fill those empty spaces,
they are truly the nursery
for love's seeds to grow.
Love's delicate flower can never flourish
in a tangled undergrowth of thought.
A silent space must be prepared for the seed
to mature and blossom
in the sanctuary of your heart.

Perceive the nature of the musk deer,
searching vainly in the forest
for the fragrance it carries within.
You too may have looked deeply
into the tangled forest of mind
to discover a meaning to your life.
Move inwards toward your heart,
with affirmations of deep acceptance and trust,
all you have feared will surely fade
when the immortal witness to the ever changing
panorama of life is discovered within.
Remember always,
this being lives only in an abundance of light,
knowing little of conditioned mind's long journey
through the dark forest.

*Craft traversing sea and sky
must utilize navigational aids
enabling them to safely reach their destination.
On life's journey too, feelings are available
as a most powerful direction finder to guide you
on an ascending voyage of self-realization.
Listen attentively to your inner feelings,
they are surely aligned with your true destiny.
Follow them with courage
and accept their accuracy.
They will guide you safely
across the stormy seas of emotion,
to the peaceful harbour of your soul.*

Light carries no memories of the darkness.
Dawn has no debt to discharge to the sunset.
Past no longer remains of any significance
to those who travel to the shore
of spiritual awareness.
The ferryman has been paid for your journey.
Your voyage across life's swiftly flowing river
may often seem perilous,
but when fears are faced courageously,
fear no longer remains a barrier
to your inner journey.
There is no need to wait,
you can at any time,
in a moment of deep meditation,
cross life's river
to the further shore of your being.
The smallest movement of consciousness
is all that is required
to experience the beauty of the further shore.

Dance lightly on the earthly stage
with footsteps that express
the deep love filling your heart.
Let stars become spotlights
illuminating the glory of your performance.
Life's ballet
will then be of the greatest excellence,
bringing joy, not only to you,
but also to those sharing your life.
When you enter the auditorium
of the magical moment, the past will disappear;
nor should the future share your stage,
for the future exists only
in the mist of your dreams.
In the moment, you will know who you truly are;
a child of eternity born from stars,
seeking to share their divine radiance with you.

There may seem to be many adversaries
opposing the way you have chosen.
Always remember, though,
they are master teachers,
enabling you to discover
and move through weaknesses,
finding your true strength.
But strength without love is of little avail,
until it can be taken to your heart.
Here it can be magically transformed into love;
a love you can share with those teachers
who have helped so surely on your way to Truth.

At each given moment a new life can commence,
when past attitudes are viewed
in the light of a new awareness.
With this knowing,
magical transformations can take place.
There are many who will say
the past cannot be changed,
but this is simply not true.
Attitude is a most powerful weapon
you can wield at any time
to cut away residual pain of past experiences.
Remember also,
the future viewed through a screen of past pain,
will inevitably be dimmed by your fear.

Fight not with the shadows
nor retain them in darkened realms
of your being.
In the light of awareness,
they will disappear like dewdrops
in the hot morning sun.

An organism tossed from the sea
to perish on an unfriendly beach,
tells of inability to adapt to change.
Nature is forever bountiful,
creating multitudes of life forms,
for she knows many will inevitably expire
in a changing environment.
As levels of consciousness rise
in the human race,
creation can only manifest
those possessing an inherent ability
to adapt to changing conditions.
Preparations are being made for souls to enter
new kingdoms of light now being formed.
It therefore becomes of vital importance
to imbibe the quality of light
into all aspects of your being.

True prayer is never a dialogue.
True prayer is a breath of gratitude to the One
for the wondrous gift of life.
The mountains are your temples,
the green grass your prayer mat,
stars you holy candles,
and sky the ultimate heaven
you long for so deeply.
There are no words or prayer to be uttered,
only a deep sigh of wonderment
when you breathe nature's beauty
into your heart.
See how willing she is
to bestow her gifts upon you.
Will you not now join her sacred dance?

Life is woven into a pattern by your dreams.
Those dreams may be of gold, love,
or even spiritual attainments.
A throne in an earthly palace
or a throne in heaven
are the very same dream,
it is of small consequence;
if you are a seeker of truth.
Truth can be found always in your awakenings,
seldom in your dreams.
Reality does not exist within the fabric of illusion,
but in the undeniable presence of the dreamer.
Remember, the dreamer can awaken
at any moment
to find the search has been in vain.
The search, in truth, was for the seeker!

Although the blessing of true love
can never be destroyed,
it can easily be forgotten.
The re-discovery may be made
in the space of self-remembrance.
Within your own heart
lies an abundance of love,
a love that can be found at any moment;
life's divine gift to share.
Do not seek to fill your empty spaces,
for in these spaces,
you can discover and celebrate your true self.
When you re-discover true self,
you will no longer ask for love.

You may use the creative faculty of imagination
to weave artistic patterns
for adorning the outer walls of your dwelling.
Admire their quality and their beauty,
but the inner walls of your dwelling
require no artistic adornment.

*Your life has been blessed
with much colour.
May that colour continue to lighten your
way as you face the journey ahead.
You have surely assisted many spirits in
their quest for light, and the love you
found will become your beacon to guide
you safely onwards.
Face the future with trust and courage,
with no regrets for the past, knowing in
your heart that to live life fully is the only
true divine purpose.*

*You have tasted the outer layers of the fruit from
life's tree.
Was it not both bitter and sweet?
Perhaps now is the time
to go deeper into its essence.
This essence can be found everywhere,
awaiting the call of light from above.
Have you not heard the song of love
on the simple sound of summer breeze,
drunk love from a cool mountain stream,
tasted love in the sweetness of forest fruits,
and felt the warmth of love
when a heart melts into you?
Go deeply into these experiences;
your life will surely be transformed
by the magic of love's alchemy.*

Light is the only true religion,
love is the only prayer,
and kindness the only ritual.
From light, all was created
and love was surely the birth
of the very first awakening in a human heart.
Go with kindness, gentleness ,and understanding;
firstly, for yourself and then for those
who stumble so helplessly
through the darkness of their night.
Remember always,
in kindness your hand becomes
the hand of the One.
Use that hand to carry
a torch light into their world,
help them to accept their own self-worth
as you surely discover yours.

The guardian of your fears
stands at the doorway to your being.
This seemingly formidable defender
appears to obstruct your way
when you endeavor to enter
your inner kingdom.
The custodian of fear echoes many threats,
attempting to deter you from your true mission.
Perhaps you may be tempted to return
to the hazardous pathway you have traveled
so many times before.
But wait, there may be new dangers to face,
far more menacing
than the ones already encountered.
Pay no heed to fear's threats...
they are meaningless and empty.
You may cross the threshold easily at any time.
Look now... you hold the key,
but there is no doorway!

*Seeking to enjoy the adoration of another
may only bring a short fulfillent.
But when another passes the garden of your
heart where blossoms flourish
in their own glory, surely they will enter
to imbibe the essence of your flowers.
Nuture your inner blooms with love.
Perceive this love as a deep acceptance
of who you really are at all times.
Your garden will then truly radiate
with the most wondrous colours of creation.*

When a real bouquet of love is presented,
celebrate each moment of its presence.
Imbibe its magic essence
into the deepest chambers of your heart,
for soon it may disappear
into the mists of earthly time.
Remember, each flower must die
so its seeds may grow into a new blossom.
There are many plastic roses
seeming to last forever;
but where is their beauty,
where is their perfume,
and where is their essence?
Rejoice in all that is real,
remembering purest reality
is also your own truth.

Remember, those choosing to return
must show great courage,
for condensed past experiences
may again be presented for direct confrontation.
Returning peaceful warriors
wield only the sword of light.
They need no armour for protection
save the shining shield of love
proudly carried in their hearts.
The peaceful warrior fights only for truth.
Know deeply,
you are the very truth your warrior fights for.

There are many so-called guides
who have not discovered their own inner light.
They attempt to lead others
to a so-called promised land.
Be wary though; they may only lead
to the edge of a deep dark chasm.
The children of light must open their eyes
and follow only the dictates of their own hearts
or they may fall again
into the darkened valley of soul's rebirth.
Use every moment of awareness
to dispel all that brings promises
for the morrow.
Remember always...
Love never promises, Love only gives.

*The quickening dawn
spreads across the horizon of a new era.
Now it is of the utmost importance
to re-discover your inner light.
When we speak of light, it is no mythical light,
but a deep knowing of your habitat
long before entry into realms of earth.
Was not the world in which you now dwell
once joined to the great star you call the sun?
You are a seed born of that same radiant light.
Since earliest awakenings of human
consciousness, man has lifted his head
toward the skies.
Firstly, to worship the great star
and then toward mythical gods
living in legends of the past.
In truth, the search is only for light;
then to discover the very same energy
manifesting as love in each human heart.
Yes, this is the true search
and also the cause of deep unrest.
Until the discovery of inner light is made,
there can be no true peace. This is spirit's
search through eons of time.*

Past has served its purpose well.
Did not the most fearsome storms
strengthen fragile shoots of wisdom,
springing forth from the dark earth
to bravely face the unknown?
There may still be times when past will attempt
to draw its seeds back into the soil.
Remember though,
you are not a time bound creature
imprisoned in nocturnal caverns of earth,
but a multi-dimensional being;
a child of eternity
existing also within boundless spheres of light.

Love knows its own name.
When you cry out from the depths of your heart
your voice is clearly heard.
Now may be the time to call out
for your true needs.
Do not deny yourself the blessings
you so willingly give to others.
Love is your beginning,
your birthright, and your destiny.
Never doubt love's presence;
it awaits patiently
on the threshold of you being for your call.
Open your heart to love,
allow the patient visitor to silently enter.

How wonderful is the word?
Can it not become an unseen flower
reaching out in space to touch another?
Let your words become bouquets of love
gathered from the garden of your heart.
Words can truly bring light
when they are spoken with love.
Always be sure your words are true,
empty words are like dead leaves,
they fall to earth soon to be forgotten.
Remember also...
a word can become a sharp sword of
destruction.
Use words with wisdom
they surely possess a great potency.
In moments of silence,
listen for the silent word echoing in your heart.
It is the echo of the very first sound
that awakened a darkened world to love.

When Sadness comes,
know that Sadness is the faithful servant of Joy,
drawing emotion from the deepest well
of your heart,
so tender seeds of love
may be watered by your tears.
But see how swiftly Sadness can return to Joy
telling his master of your readiness to receive him!

Look not back in anger nor forward in fear.
When you cast your head over your shoulder,
perceive the past only with understanding
and a deep acceptance of all that was presented.
Nor should you fear the future;
for fear multiplies its own energy many times,
creating a fertile field for its dark seeds to grow;
eventually manifesting
that which you fear so much.
There is naught to fear but fear itself.
Allow the light of awareness to
shine on past events;
listening attentively to the wisdom
of your inner guide.
Each new day will then surely be adorned
by the most magnificent colours of creation.

Would you reproach winds of change
so lovingly carrying a sheltered seed
away from the darkness to flourish in the light?
Neither can you cast judgment on the storms
that give so much strength
to a plant's fragile stem.
Remember always, each flower grows
in its own way and in its own season.
Meditate within your own garden,
but do not close your eyes.
Nature surely can be seen
as your wisest teacher.
Perceive how each plant grows in its own glory,
no roseflower longing to become a lily
or weeping willow desiring
to become a mighty oak.

Spirit sails upon a vast ocean
of pure consciousness;
an ancient mariner flying
toward the bright star of his destiny.
There may be times when you feel winds of
change are diverting you from your true course
but as you cast your vision
away from earth, into the vast heavens,
you will surely discover the light of your star
guiding you safely on your homeward voyage.
Raise your vision towards the open sky.
Perceive the graceful flight of a dove
and the splendour of a golden eagle
ascending towards highest summits.
Surely their flight depends upon
a perfect harmony of wings.
Can you in all pervading wisdom,
conceive such flights
propelled by a single wing?
A single wing would certainly imprison
these poor creatures within an earthly habitat,
never to experience the exhilaration
of wide open heavens.
In human life also, a deep harmony can be found
within the seeming duality of existence,
enabling you to ascend
to the very peak of your being.

Forgive and remember who you truly are.
Perhaps deepest wounds of the past
are but affronts to an illusory ego.
But you are not your ego,
you are not your mind,
and you are certainly not your body.
In truth you are a far greater dimension.
When you remember who you truly are,
there will be much for giving.
What greater gift can you give but love?
In your remembrance you will surely find
an abundance of this eternal quality to share
with those who you feel have harmed you.
Love is the most potent healer.
When you share your light with another,
your own wounds become magically healed
by its powerful energy.

True love may not be discovered
until you have encountered and discarded
that which was not meant to be yours.
Past has served its purpose well
but now is the time to bid it farewell
with a deep sigh of gratitude.
Send out your invitations to souls
who can now bring joy to your heart.
True love will then surely blossom
in the new light illuminating your world.

*Life's great illusion
is the dream that you are apart from others.
In truth this is not possible.
You may feel alone,
but in meditative awareness,
this feeling can be transformed
into a totally different dimension of being.
In deep awareness you realize
that each particle in our vast universe,
is interdependent upon all others,
joined inextricably by the common bond of love.
Now in this silent space,
you can discover your truth.
Here the totality of the universe is yours
and you also are the total universe.*

There are many illusions
arrayed on the stage of mind.
Dwell not upon that which will surely change...
remember always,
while scene shifters perform their worldly task,
you can step into the auditorium at any time
to witness...
dramas, tragedies,and comedies
that will surely pass.
When you are called forth to play a role,
perform it to the best of your ability
and heart will truly applaud your performance.

Some spiritual practices
may seem to bring a temporary relief
from the incessant turmoil of life,
but a constant vigilance becomes necessary.
The wolf in the guise of spirituality
may be a far greater danger
than direct confrontation
with the reality of your fears.
When fears are viewed through real eyes
they often disappear, leaving space
for true growth of your spirit.

Perceive how life's flowing river
inevitably wends its way
towards the vast ocean.
Although its direction
may at times seem diverse,
river's route is predetermined
by forces of nature.
Perhaps your routes
often appear to be diverse,
seemingly leading away from a chosen path,
but it is not wise to fight
with the wisdom of the river...
relax into its flow,
it will surely carry you effortlessly
to the boundless ocean of the One.

Past appears before you now as a harbinger,
bringing a most important summary of your life.
Do not dismiss the messenger
until you have listened carefully to his voice,
or he will surely return to haunt your dreams.
Perceive past now with understanding,
each situation, each person, and each
experience.
Greet your messenger with love and gratitude,
for he has truly traveled far
to be with you today.

You are the architect of your world.
When you acknowledge that
past thoughts and attitudes
have created your present environment,
you will surely realize
a new life can commence this very moment.
This is one of life's greatest discoveries.
Remember always,
you are part of divine creation;
surely creation has blessed you
with the very same ability.
In awareness of this gift,
you will know in your heart
you can design a new world,
using the magical power of thought.

When you enter the mystery,
the mystery of a magical moment,
past disappears.
Past exists only in its own memories.
Future neither can share your moment.
Future appears only
through the mists of your dreams.
This divine mystical moment is a tender child,
born from a vast eternity,
where your soul has always lived.
In this sacred space,
a doorway opens to your inner temple;
enter now and discover who you really are.

Protection takes many forms.
Does not the husk protect a fragile seed
from the consuming intensity of the sun?
And does not mother earth draw seed
into the warm soil of her heart
to nurture her child?
But protection must eventually be discarded
when light beckons seed from the dark soil.
There may be many dangers
when first shoots emerge from seed's tiny heart.
For there are many, who in ignorance
would destroy fragile new growth.
Seed can do naught but trust, though,
in the light calling it forth from earth.
This is the very nature of life
and also the story of your own awakening.
Open your heart in trust
and let your seed discover
the blessing of a new dawn.
You will surely become a most magnificent
blossom on life's ever abundant tree of love.

Truth requires no support.
Truth stands alone unaided and
cannot be questioned or dismissed.
Frequently, though,
truth poses a great threat to your dreams,
dreams that seem so comfortable and real.
Always remember,
dreams can often obscure light from your eyes
if you are a seeker of truth.

Enjoy the restful peace of the valley,
marveling at the flowers and listening silently
to nature's voice within her trees.
Accept with thankfulness guides
who have shown the way to your valley.
Rest for a while in the shade
and let spirit become recharged
by the healing touch of nature's hand.
When you ascend the mountain again,
take the beauty of your valley with you.

*Use deep awareness
to bring past to a vantage point,
where it may be seen clearly
from the pinnacle of your being.
When you look down
upon life's swiftly flowing river
from your mountain top,
past will miraculously dissolve
into the pure water of the river.
You may see this as a cleansing process,
but in truth, all that is required
is clear observation, without judgment.
Perceive how lingering memories
have formed dark clouds over your sun.
Now in the space of a new awareness,
your inner sun can burst forth from the clouds
in golden splendour.*

Freedom is love's very nature.
Love does not imprison
ascending songbirds in golden cages,
nor harness beasts of burden
to carry heavy loads upon their back.
Conditioned mind may make many illusory
prisons, preventing your spirit
from ascending or may have promised
a golden heaven in some remote realm.
But we say in truth,
when mind's cage door is opened...
you are already there.

A star is born as another one dies,
yet the old continues to shine its light
into a world of time,
giving an illusion of an existing reality.
Know deeply, life is an ever renewing
phenomenon,
existing far beyond boundaries of time.
Life is a new star born
in your heart at each moment.
Once this is seen clearly,
you will know that past events,
whether you consider them to be from this life
or past incarnations, are no longer a reality.
Look deeply into your heart to find your truth
and let that truth become illuminated
by the guiding light of your new star.
As your new star shines forth,
give freely of the love you find in its light;
past will then no longer appear so real.

Doubt and uncertainty are open invitations
to enter the vast unknown.
In Truth life can never be known;
it always remains an open book,
inviting you to write your unique adventure story
on the empty sheet presented each day.
When you look back on your life,
perhaps you are tempted to transfer
pages from your past
into the volume before you.
It may seem easier,
for has not the past been indelibly inscribed
with distress and fear you have known?
We do not say, past has no value,
but why not write of joy and happiness
in the light you have found?
Write each new page with wisdom
and colour it with love,
knowing it is a unique unlimited edition.

Move inward toward your heart
with affirmations of deep acceptance and trust.
Fears will then fade
when the immortal witness to the ever changing
panorama of your life is found.
This is true meditation.
The only authentic quest,
to discover and honor the eternal self.
Remember, this being lives only
in an abundance of light,
knowing little of the darkness of your journey.
Accept all you find,
remembering always,
the impartial witness does not reside
in a judgmental mind
but in the light temple of your heart.

Perhaps when you look into your heart,
you discover a deep sadness.
You may have clung so tightly to laws of mind,
that heart has been denied fruit from life's tree.
Heart's hands can no longer reach out
to imbibe the essence of tree's fruit.
Did you not see them falling to earth uneaten?
Perhaps your heart is hungry,
having been denied
the sustenance of love and freedom.
These are truly the sweetest fruits
to be sampled from life's ever abundant tree.
Examine all that does not bring joy
into your heart.
Remember, there is always an open invitation
to a most magnificent banquet.
Look within, your table has been prepared.

In giving we become instruments of the divine.
When you truly give your heart to another,
you have given your heart to the One.
When you touch another with tenderness,
know it is the hand of the One
touching in tenderness.
And is not light in your eyes also a beacon
guiding other travelers
to the healing sanctuary of the One
so their maladies may be healed
by the light of divine love?
In giving and sharing your gifts unselfishly
you are but a procreator of divine energy.
Could there be a greater purpose to your life?

Conditioned mind is your genie,
with a mysterious magical lamp,
promising to fulfill your deepest desires.
When dreams appear to contain degrees of
reality, does not the genie inevitably return
inviting you to ask for greater gifts?
In truth, it is you who will become the slave,
the slave of mind and its insatiable desires.
Would you not wish to become free
from this cruel master?
When you move into your heart
you will open the gateway to freedom,
where mind's influence can no longer
become a diversion from self-discovery.

You may have been led by others
on certain pathways
that seemed most attractive.
Your eyes, however, have been given
so you may truly see your own way ahead.
There are many signposts on your journey;
stop for a while to read their directions,
but move on in trust to find your own way.
There may seem to have been
many cul-de-sacs on your journey,
but did you not discover flowers by the wayside?
Remember, each soul's journey is unique,
a pathway of discovery
into the very depths of your heart.

*All that lives dies
and all that dies is reborn.
That is the immutable law of life.
Death is but the pillow in the cradle of life.
As a child awakens in awareness,
the pillow is left behind
and fears of death or dying
can no longer obscure the light of reality.
In your heart you know,
you are neither body nor mind.
They are but manifestations of a far deeper reality;
an eternal dimension of creativity
existing simultaneously on many levels.*

When nature's season enters a new phase,
winds of change will surely take many seeds
towards more fertile soil.
Her purpose seems very clear.
Are you also not a seed of nature?
Relax into changes occurring in your life
and you will surely find the soil
that will truly nurture your growth.
Attune to the wisdom of the flowers and trees,
and trust in Nature's love,
caring so deeply for her tiny seeds.
When the blossoming of your consciousness
occurs, share its flowers so their seeds may
grow in fertile fields of other hearts.
It is then that your life will be truly blessed.

In an orchestra many instruments combine
to express the creativity of composer
and talents of each musician.
In many respects, life too is a vast orchestra.
If you seek a performance of the highest quality,
all frequencies and talents
must be combined in harmony,
in the presentation of your symphony.
Surely the symphony would not be complete
should strings be dismissed
and equally if percussion were absent,
much would be lost.
All can be used in your rendition.
Life's lower levels are expressed
in base instruments.
Higher self is represented by upper frequencies.
It is true your symphony may have been written
many lives ago but remember,
a new one can be scored at any moment.
Perform each new masterpiece
with great excellence.

Disease, pain and suffering
are surely fed by the energy of guilt.
Guilt is not, as you may believe, a feeling,
but suppression of a feeling.
In truth that feeling is love.
Know in your heart, love can transcend all,
every thought and every feeling of unworthiness.
Love requires only a deep surrender.
There is no perfection to be achieved,
no recriminations, or regrets for past events,
only a gift of love for yourself.
In acceptance of this reality,
a deep healing can take place on all levels.

The fragrance of nature's earthly garden
is truly sweet.
Surely she has many blessings
to bestow upon her children.
Light is the greatest of all.
Whilst all others must inevitably be returned,
light is yours forever.
Light is the farewell gift you may take
when you leave the physical form
and it is also the energy
to transform your life now.

No matter what

No matter what they tell us, no matter what they do, no matter what they teach us, what we believe is true. No matter what they call us, how ever they attack, no matter where they take us, we'll find our own way back. I can't deny what I believe, I can't be what I'm not, I'll know our love forever, I know no matter what. If only tears were laughter, if only night was day, if only prayers were answered, then we would hear God say, no matter what they tell you, no matter what they teach you, what you believe is true, and I will keep you safe and strong, and sheltered from the storm, no matter where it's barren, a dream is being born. No matter who they follow, no matter where they lead, no matter how they judge us, I'll be everyone you need. No matter if the sun don't shine, or if the skies are blue, no matter what the ending, my life began with you. I can't deny what I believe, I can't be what I'm not, I know this loves forever, I know no matter what, I can't deny what I believe, I can't be what I'm not. I know this loves forever, that's all that matters now - no matter what.

Perhaps when you read these words
you will remember;
not a memory stored
in the cellular structure of your brain,
but a memory in your heart,
A memory of a silent space,
where an agreement was made
to return and help
brothers and sisters seeking light.
Remembrance in your heart is all we ask
and remembrance is the point
from where great changes can occur.

Dawn has no imagination, sunset no regrets.
They exist purely in their own reality,
their own truth.
There are no dreams, hopes or regrets
in their structure.
Surely it is a world of fantasy
placing heavy burdens upon your back.
We do not say you should not dream,
but let your dreams tell of the golden light
of your awakening.
When clouds seem to indicate an imminent
storm, take them to your heart,
dispel their darkness with your love.
Look now towards the horizon,
see how clear is the sky of your new dawn.

*Outer pathways
have been traversed many times
on life's seemingly never ending journey.
There are many signposts
indicating directions others have traveled,
and their adventures have been well recorded
in chronicles of time.
You may feel an affinity with them,
following them for a while,
but they can never lead to your own truth.
That truth patiently awaits your discovery
when you embark on your unique adventure,
a journey to the sacred temple of your heart.
It is true you may encounter many obstacles
when you move inwards; they may seem even
more menacing than those fears you left behind.
Your fears, however, are but guardians enlisted
by a lower mind,
preventing all but the fearless from entry
to the inner temple of your being.
Move inwards with trust,
shining a new awareness
upon all you encounter.*

Perhaps there are conditions
you would gladly seek to change ,
but this may not be possible.
With acceptance of a greater wisdom,
alignment takes place with divine intelligence.
All must eventually accept and surrender
to the natural flow of life's river,
inevitably wending its way
to a mighty ocean of energy.
Although you may dream
you are a droplet in that river,
one day you will awaken to discover...
you are the mighty ocean.

Follow fearlessly the dream in your heart,
although it may be a dream
created in a long forgotten existence.
That dream will still lead you towards
your inner temple of truth.
When you arrive at your temple,
there will be no acclaim for your success,
naught to be conquered, naught to be achieved.
Only the realization of your dream.

*Close your eyes... rest awhile... breathe
quietly... look within... acknowledge your
thoughts without judgment... allow mind's
activity to reduce slowly, a magical
transformation scene will then take place...
The golden carriage of a magical moment
appears to take you to a magnificent celebration
taking place in your honor. This celebration is
in the silent ballroom of your heart. You will not
have to find a partner to share your dance for
each particle in our vast universe eagerly awaits
your arrival. Join them joyfully in the magic of
their eternal dance.*

*Masks of persona create a deep illusion of
reality imprisoning spirit in a world of time.
Now in this very moment
you can reclaim your true identity
in realms of creativity.
Creativity is not born from time;
it belongs to something far greater,
the vastness of your being, living in light.
Do you not see light shining forth
from an artist's canvas
or perceive the beauty of creation's dawn?
In light and love you can discover creativity.
Lift blankets of illusion;
awaken your creative eternal child now,
from its slumber in the cradle of time.
Hear its joyous greeting
when you enter the nursery of heart
to reclaim a child you had forgotten.*

In fear, spirit shrinks into a shell of protection.
Whilst fear may be useful to protect physical
body on its earthly journey, it can do naught but harm
festering under the name of protection.
Here it divides and multiplies,
producing many more seemingly real illusions
to capture and imprison a fearful spirit
in darker caverns.
Remember light and darkness can never cohabit,
neither can fear and love
share the same dwelling.
Have no fear when you awaken each day,
know in your heart many guides
walk beside you in love.
Know also, as you sleep
their light will surely shine
on the pathway of your dreams.

The loving gardener experiences much joy
as the seed he has planted
matures and blossoms
in Nature's bountiful garden.
We too rejoice as we see seeds of light planted
within the earth mature and blossom
with utmost grandeur.
Without the quality of love,
this growth could not be possible.
Remember always,
each touch of love and each breath
of gratitude are the true sustenance
of your flowers.
Whilst seeds belong to the earth and must return,
their blossoms are yours to keep forever.

The silent song of dawn enraptures night
with her sweet music.
See how lovingly darkness melts into her arms?
From this love song a new day is born.
Enter the Sacred Temple of Dawn
with great reverence to receive your blessings.
Imbibe the essence of nature's garden
beholding a vast congregation
assembled before you.
Creatures of earth, air, and water bring their
gifts to share each new day.
Join them joyfully in their sacred dance
celebrating light's eternal blessing.
Surely then, love will light a holy candle
within your heart to carry with you
when night returns once more.

You have gathered many wild flowers
from the wayside on your journey,
but see how those flowers have now withered
in the bright sun of your new day.
Surely the intensity of this new light
will hasten the demise of yesterday's blossoms
plucked from their earthly roots.
The old must be shed
if space is to be found for new flowers of this day
to be carried in your heart.

Life is an embarkation on a voyage of discovery,
a journey to find a golden treasure
that has been lost.
This bounty is in truth, a part of yourself,
a part that has become separated
by tempests of time's turbulent ocean.
The deepest yearning in the heart
is but the awakening of a memory
stirring from distant echoes of past.
The search for love
is surely born from that memory.
True love is the ultimate discovery
of your own treasure trove in another heart.
Your quest may seem to present many hazards
while you cross the vast ocean, but sail bravely on,
knowing in your heart your voyage
has been carefully planned
by the Master Mariner of your destiny.
Yes, true love is the culmination of a search
for your soul mate.
May the love you find,
guide you safely to the tranquil haven of heart.

The whisper within your heart that calls thee,
is an echo of a promise made long ago
in the timeless silent space of light's kingdom.
Surely this voice tells of the light you have forgotten and
the inner peace
your heart once knew.
Bethink though, you promised to return
to tell others of the glory of this realm
where they once dwelt.
When you illuminate their dark earthly caverns
with the light you will find,
surely these dwellings can become
most radiant temples of glory.

What is the deepest desire in your heart?
If that desire is for light
you must surely open your eyes,
for there are many who may endeavor at this time
to lure you to the edge of a dangerous
precipice, where, with closed eyes,
you will again fall into the earthly valley
of soul's rebirth.
Work only with light, but do not draw light
from any earthly well.
It may seem to sparkle with reflections of the sky,
but it can possess no ascending quality.
Let your life be gauged only by the amount of
light you can pour into your heart.
It is only when your own heart is brimming over
with light, you can perceive the gateway
to love's enchanted garden...
the garden your heart remembers.

You are no stranger in paradise.
You have shared the garden of paradise with
many of your family, but perhaps that time has
been forgotten. Did you not sleep so deeply
beneath the wondrous tree of life?
It is true, you dreamt of its blossoms and fruit;
they seemed so near, but when you reached out,
the fruit disappeared. Now as you truly awaken
you will see the fruit you sought for so long,
has always been there, an aspect of reality
not of your dreams.
See how blue is the sky in heart's enchanted
garden and how playfully creatures of earth
touch your hand.
Marvel also at the tree which sheltered you
whilst you slept. Perceive how it also stretches
so lovingly to reach the sun you longed for so
deeply. As the dream ends,
there will be much joy in your heart.
Now no search to be made, no path to take,
no tool to make heart's garden more perfect.
Enjoy the immense beauty of your blossoms and
sample the goodness of the fruit your tree bears.
Has it not waited so long to become part of you?

In the space of silence, a deep yearning arises,
to know who you are.
It is true, mind will penetrate your silence
by providing many false identities,
derived from false beliefs and conditioning.
But none of these are really true.
You have collected a vast wardrobe
from many earthly incarnations
and have worn them both shamefully and with
great pride. In the search for true self they must
be cast aside.
The precious diamond lies deeply in the earth
and outer coverings have to be removed
before the beauty of its perfection
can be perceived.
Recognize your truest nature.
In love you know who you are.
In love, no outer coverings are required,
false personalities are cast away;
like worn clothes from past journeys,
they are left by the wayside.

*In times of chaos trust in the
wisdom of the One.
Remember, it is from chaos
a star is born.
Even in the deepest chaos
you can discover
an infinite perfection at work
binding all with the common bond
of love.*

You may have fallen in love,
though all that truly falls is the illusory ego.
In deepest love, ego must fall away
to reveal the essence of the One you truly are.
When love opens your heart
there may be much pain,
for ego does not surrender willingly
to the light it has not seen for so long.
But with the blessings of true love,
deep wounds of the past will be magically healed
when they are exposed to the new light you will
find within.

In relationship,
a deep desire to retain your beloved
is quite natural,
for did not your beloved bring those wonder
filled moments of joy,
happiness, and bliss to capture your heart?
To love another is a great benediction,
but love must find its own freedom,
in its own space, and in its own time.
When a loved one is surrendered,
you are alone in your totality
to discover who you truly are.
When this discovery is made,
a beacon is magically lit within
to guide another to the open doorway
of your heart.

When words can no longer quench your thirst,
cast your gaze away
from tangled undergrowth of intellect;
look upwards towards the light,
meditating deeply on the nature of the sky.
Sky touches all but never penetrates,
yet its substance is infinite
and cannot be contained.
Sky is the canvas for artists rainbow
and also the father of the raging storm.
Sky is the backdrop for Mother Natures
earthly scenario
and also the pathway to heaven's stars.
Sky is the carrier of unseen communication
and the home of raindrops
that will touch the rose with love.
Sky creates space for the darkest clouds and
makes way for the brilliance
of the noonday sun.
Sky touches the deepest recesses of your heart
and the farthest galaxies in our vast universe.
Meditate on these things
and bring peace to your heart.

Human mind can rarely become the fertile soil
for spiritual growth,
but it can often smother and stifle
the fragile seed
so earnestly seeking the blessings of light.
Remember always,
it may not be necessary to go too deeply
into phenomena that can be of little value
to spirit's ascension.
In a world where many
compelling manifestation
of the strangest nature seem to occur,
mind will attempt to dig deeply into its archives
searching for reasons and explanations.
Do not concern yourself too strongly with reason,
those who would seek the light
must stay close to the surface of mind.
If seeds are planted too deeply,
they may not grow.
Remember, nearer to the surface,
you are closer to the light!

Love gives and love takes away.
Love takes away many illusions
created by the ever changing phenomena
of your world,
so you may percieve the unchanging essence
of who you truly are.
In love you will not discover your mind,
for love knows naught of reason
and mind knows naught of love.
Love's purpose lies within its own fulfillment
and the propagation of its seeds
within our vast universe.

*We speak now of forgiveness and the role it
plays in healing. Although it may not be
apparent, forgiveness of yourself
is also forgiveness of others.
What greater gift do you truly have for giving
other than the divine quality of love?
In forgiveness you remember you are part of the
whole as the illusion of separation is dispelled.
To heal a heart on the deepest level
requires the highest degree of awareness.
Although many maladies of the physical body
seem to manifest a multitude of symptoms,
they all seem to be related to past events in some way.
In an event or action that requires forgiveness,
the circumstances or times are of
little importance, for in the very act of
forgiveness a deep healing can take place
on many levels.
But we speak not of a few words of empty apology;
no, it is something far greater...
when you share the love and light
you can surely find in your own heart,
you are truly giving.*

Love cannot be defined
it is boundless,
like the vast sky
it touches everything,
holding nothing
but its own essence.
Love is the silent song
of your soul
calling thee
to share her music.
Love sings her poetry for you,
but when your cup runneth over
with its nectar
it can refresh many arid tongues.

All pathways lead to the light.
In the beginning it is the light of understanding
that dawns on the horizon
of human consciousness.
Understanding can be conveyed
mostly by words.
The first dawn becomes eventually lost
in the brilliance of the day
when sun steeps
towards her zenith.
Understanding then grows
into the tree of knowing.
Trust is the leaf on the stem and love is the
ultimate blossom.
This truly is your pathway, your journey,
and your destination...
there can be no other.

*Thoughts, dreams, and images
are but shadowy clouds of mind
drifting through your blue sky.
Observe their movement following only those
bringing joy to your heart.
Condemning or judging the process of thought
may create many obstacles
in your quest for peace.
In judgment sorrow is born.
Perceive mind's magical pictures impartially
and let their clouds drift by in your ever present sky.
Seek not to live within the clouds
or they may never pass to reveal the sunlight.*

*Perceive the true reflection of
your inner mirror.
It can be a teacher of the highest
caliber.
But if you do not like the image
reflected,
do not break it...
it could bring the greatest misfortune
if lessons are ignored!*

Hold the torch you have been given
high above your head
so all may see and be guided by its radiance.
Perhaps your beacon has been held
too close to your breast.
Lift it towards the sky
showing the light to all who choose
to open their eyes.
A divine torch bearer can illuminate many
darkened pathways,
guiding many souls on the quest
to discover their own inner light.

Reality cannot be found in passing events,
only within awareness
of deeper levels of consciousness.
There is no situation, event, or feeling
that does not change
save the dimension existing within
to perceive the Truth.
It has been suggested that passing phenomena
are but remembered dreams
of a slumbering spirit.
Whatever you may accept or deny,
there can be little doubt
that you are the eternal witness.
You may often deny your dreams,
but how can you
deny the reality of the dreamer?

Reality can never be changed,
but the point
from which it is viewed
will always remain your choice.

*The feeble heart
has not the capacity
to experience the deepest levels
of life.
It is the strongest heart
that will feel the greatest pain.
That heart beats deeply in tune
with spirit's growth
towards it destiny.
The pain in your heart
is but the forgotten spirit
crying out for recognition.*

*Each human relationship
is a journey into your own being
not measured by distance or time
but by the depths of emotion
you feel in your heart.*

The breath of the wind
singing streams' soft music
and flower's upturned head towards the sky
can be far greater teachers
than words of scriptures found in your churches
and temples; they tell only
of another's way to realization.
To worship footprints in the sands of time
is to miss your own way.
Look not downwards towards the sand,
follow fragrant flower's example;
turn your head upwards towards the light.
Let the flowers, trees, rivers,
creatures of the air,
land, and ocean become your gurus.
They surely belong to creativity
happening now at this very moment.
Know also that you too are also an intrinsic part
of that creative process.
Transform religion into a deep reverence
for all creation and you will truly worship.

*Perceive the intricate pattern
of your life unfolding.
Although it may not be
possible to see each stitch
being woven into your canvas,
nevertheless, the weaving of
soul's garment continues
through each moment.*

*May the Light and love we have
shared together
through these pages shine forth
forever more
enlightening the hearts of those
who gaze towards our stars.*

Omano

PART II

Readings

July 8th, 1993 - Jean

Until inner light is re-awakened within spirit's heart, earthly night seems endless, while you search in vain to find the light of a new day upon the horizon of your world. In truth your outer dawn is kindled from within. When the spark of eternal life is found, a great healing of the physical body can take place; you will inevitably find you are no longer encapsulated by the darkness and fears of the morrow.

In truth, all healing comes from within and light is the medium for transmission of healing energies. Although it is true your physical body may require the diligent use of established medical practices to remove symptoms, all deep healing takes place within etheric energy fields surrounding and pervading your physical body. Perceive how Nature responds to light.

Have you not admired the beauty of spring's new blossoms? Would they be possible without the gift of light? Disease of your body may be the direct result of a depravation of light. Although maladies may be transmitted from many past lives, these conditions are presented to you now, enabling a deep healing to take place within this incarnation - on all levels - when your inner light is re-awakened. Look within and in your quiescent moments you will discover the key to unlock the dark prison in which you feel so helpless. Trust deeply in many guides - both seen and unseen - who shine their light upon your path; the way to find the peace you seek, enabling you to re-establish a deep harmony within. Use every means available to awaken and reflect your inner light, although at this moment it may be the smallest of flames. In awareness of its presence, you will find it possible to create a luminance beyond your wildest beliefs. Here, Jean, lies your true healing.

All that is real is eternal. All that is illusory will fade, with this deep awareness all imagined fears will be dispelled by the light of a new knowing. Surrender all that is unreal in your life retaining

only that which cannot be taken away and more shall be given as space is found in your heart for truth.

Love requires no light years to be measured to the stars... how can you measure the distance to your inner being?

When you pray, ask only for the gift of silence... when your mind is silent there will be naught to ask for.

You may ask the meaning of being human, I say in truth, the meaning is contained in your tears and in your laughter too. You can also find it in the silent vigil you keep through the long night, awaiting the gift of dawn's first light.

This is a reading I broadcast on South African T.V. in 1991

Whilst spirit lives a restricted life in the world of time, there will always be conflict within the human heart. In truth, man resides at a junction, on a thin dividing line between the relative world of time and the timeless eternity of the One. Only when this realization permeates human consciousness, can a life of harmony be lived. The night cannot be denied, it is joined to the day. Without death there can be no life, yet man continues to deny the polarities of cosmic and earthly worlds.

In the wider spectrum of existence the opposite can not be denied. The egocentric attitude, seeing the center of the universe as a reference point within the head or mind, seems to be the source of all worldly problems. Even in wider geographical aspects, boundaries drawn by a finite mind can never be a true focal point for existence.

Throughout the boundless universe there is a refining process in continual operation; not, however, a process moving from imperfection to perfection; no, it is from perfection to perfection. All is as it has been and always will be. Past and future will melt into the moment, when mind dissolves in meditation. The world of time and boundaries disappear as you link with the totality of life. To dwell entirely in the time of a limited earthly experience, is to sleep in the nightmarish dreams of darkness.

Beggars and kings, ministers and politicians, all share a common paupers grave; see their bodies covered by the rotting shroud of ego as they are lowered into their tomb, ideologies relinquished in death. All will disintegrate into the refining process common to all manifestations of the whole. This same law exists throughout the cosmos - does your mind perceive an exemption on earthly planes?

Pose no questions of time, you know deep down it is but an earthly measurement not existing in the wider aspects of our vast universe. Would you still choose to measure the distance between your world and the planets, whilst ignoring the journey towards your own heart? In your heart resides the answers to your questions, though in truth there are no answers, but a deep knowing, a deep trust in the totality of life.

Fear is often the template for its own manifestation.

The wheel of life may seem to turn endlessly, but see how still the hub remains. Can you not discover the very same phenomenon within?

The warrior of Truth faces his adversary with dignity and trust, needing no armour for defense but the shining shield of love he carries proudly before him. Neither does he flourish any weapon save the sharp sword of awareness he uses wisely to destroy the illusions appearing before him.

January 31, 1994

Build a temple of light from the love you find in your heart for there are many now awakening who will seek the sanctuary so their maladies may be healed before ascension to realms of light. It has been necessary to expose those who are awakening to the final dream in their sleep state. It may not be possible to discover a reason for circumstances beyond the realms of comprehension but you must trust and convey that quality of trust to those who may enter your temple. If the dream state produces a beautiful illusion of the utmost wonder and if the perfume in the garden of your dreams is of exquisite fragrance, the dreamer may never wish to awaken or to leave the wondrous garden of dreams.

It, therefore, may become necessary to produce a most fiendish nightmare, that the dreamer may be shocked into awakening. The way of the One may not be understood, but when doubts appear in your mind you have once again lost the quality of trust. It is true there are many energies of lower frequencies endeavoring to manifest into your world, but remember, they can also be used to enable the perfect law to be expressed. When darkness pervades the being, shine the powerful light in the tower of your temple to guide a lost spirit to your sanctuary. Allow the bell to ring clearly from the bell tower of your heart and make it ring so loudly that spirits' may be awakened from the nightmare they may be living in their dreams. There are many light beings manifesting in your realms, they are there to assist you in our work.

April 25, 1993

There may be deep feelings of remorse when you feel powerless to manifest conditions in your life seeming so important. Perhaps the very same feelings are there when your endeavors to help those closest to you are met with failure. In these situations life's deepest truths are often shown. Here you must surrender to a

greater will. Whilst your endeavors remain of the greatest importance to your mind they are nevertheless quite insignificant on
deeper levels. Many times have we spoken of trust and again I would
direct your awareness towards this quality. In each thought, in each
dream and in each endeavor, mind appears to be the controlling
factor behind the scenes but when your plans go awry, mind can
seldom accept defeat or surrender to a greater will. Therefore, the
quality of your trust must be constantly reviewed and renewed as
you become aware of its absence. Future can never be known, it
is beyond the capabilities of mind. Mind can only call upon
memories of experiences in the past to project its dreams into a
time dimension it calls "The future." In truth, future does not
and cannot exist. Life and truth can only be discovered in a
timeless space. Fret not for those you cannot help, their own
destiny must be fulfilled. Their deep wounds must fester and
bring forth poisons that would otherwise erode any possibility
of spiritual growth. Show them your compassion, but not your
mind; this can never be directed towards the deep wounds you
seek to heal. Nature has a far greater intelligence. Trust deeply
in her wisdom.

Perfection

Many may believe that growth towards a more perfect person is
the foremost requirement on the so-called "spiritual path". This
may, or may not be true. However, the very concept of growth is
probably the most formidable of all barriers to be penetrated on
spirit's quest for discovery of the Authentic Self within. When the
concept of becoming a more perfect human being arises, there
seems to be a great resistance to facing the negative and the fearful
side of your nature. You may strive to change this but meet with
little success. Many lives can be wasted in striving to become
what you really are, but afraid to acknowledge.
Change though, is an essential component for an inner journey to

self discovery. The change required, however, is not the ability to become a better human being, but a change of attitude, a change of mind to see life and yourself as you really are. This seeing, this awareness, must also include the seemingly realistic fears we find within our minds, the delusions and the false identities often bestowed by others. When they are seen for what they are, they magically disappear and the Authentic Self emerges from the darkness of their shadows.

November, 1991 - Claire

Love unfolds, it can never be forced. Love must inevitably commence within. There may be many subconscious wishes that will seek their own fulfillment and it is necessary to acknowledge them in their own sphere. Always remember, that you are not your mind, that must be your conscious meditation. Mind makes a good servant, but a bad master and the process of mind control must be gradually eliminated before you can experience the natural harmony with life that your spirit longs for so deeply. Depression and unhappiness can be valuable tools for introspection, though that introspection must not divide, separate, or judge the pictures that are viewed. Life must change and unhappiness is necessary to tell you that happiness and harmony are being suppressed. Pain becomes the body's signal that all is not well, and likewise, unhappiness will indicate that you are not in alignment with the natural flow of life. You may choose to listen or to ignore; life though, will continue manifesting in natural laws that cannot be changed. Attitudes must be aligned with life, not with your mind which will lead you away from the light into the darkest caverns. Develop the divine quality of intuition, a great teaching that comes from the deeper knowing within.

Seek not your fulfillment from outside sources, they will eventually cause disappointment and unhappiness. Each spirit must fulfill their own destiny, which can never be changed. As the

light in your life shines ever brighter much will be revealed by
its rays. Enjoy what you have, seek that which only your heart
decides, remembering that true love can never come from mind.
You must let go of many things which are craved by mind, they
were never meant to belong to you. True love never possesses, it
only gives. You have given much, though not enough to the thirsty
spirit within. Nurture your spirit with the nectar of love and the
false expectations will fade. The light will burn ever brighter when
the power of true love is found within.

November 12, 1991 - Mary

There is much beauty in life's garden, though spirit's seed must be
tended and nurtured before the blossom of love bursts forth in all
its wondrous colour and glory. The fragile seed of love can be found
everywhere and in all beings. You are a gardener of life when you
tend the seed in those you touch. How proud the gardener is when
the fruit of his labors matures. As in the natural process of life,
when alignment is made with natural forces, much guidance and
knowing is given. When you open your heart in a love that requires
naught, many blessings are bestowed. A closed heart cannot grow
for it will turn to stone, an open heart blooms in its own right.
Perhaps it is time to cease seeking the meaning of life. Have you
not found it in the beauty of your human garden? Love is the only
gift that we can request from life, and we must first develop the
capacity to love and accept ourselves, then we have much more to
give as Nature's energy multiplies within our fountain of love.
This is the fountain that overflows to make your spiritual garden
more fertile. You will touch many with your gift. Trust in the
divine power of that gift and more will be given, for we too rejoice
in the glory of abundant blossoms in our garden.

November 12, 1991

Man is a bridge, a bridge that exists between the unconscious and the conscious. There are many evolutionary paths leading to the bridge. Time spent upon the pathways in Truth has no reality. In reality time does not exist. In truth there is no time. In the awakened one, there is a no conflict between the real and the unreal, the conscious and the unconscious. The awakened one will see that man is a meeting point, not a conflict of energy. Life's reality lies only in awakening; the bridge is the medium for that transformation. To become awakened is to move forward on the evolutionary cycle. Whilst you live in mind there will always appear a choice. When you live consciously your energy will merge with natural evolution. Perceive the intricacies of the pattern, can you not see the rock melting into the star and the dreamer awakening in the human heart?

The light of awareness to be re-awakened is the only requirement for your truth to be revealed...but:

Search not for the secrets of the Weaver whilst the wondrous woven pattern of the Weaver's mystery is displayed within you.

Unnecessary shoots of knowledge may have to be pruned from your mind allowing the flower of knowing to flourish more abundantly in your heart!

Despair can become a doorway to Truth when the heavy curtain of fear is drawn back to reveal the light.

November 1, 1991 - Christine

There is a great restlessness in the heart and it is good. Look not for peace in your mind, it can never be found. Ride on the crest of emotion and the journey will take you to your heart. In mind there can be no fulfillment and love can find no fertile soil for its growth. In restlessness you are encouraged to find peace, but your journey to the heart center must first be completed. Bring your own light into all that you do and a greater insight will be bestowed upon you. There is but one true journey in life and it must be followed fearlessly trusting in all that is presented. Use the energy of your restlessness to discover your true peace, remembering that all reflected relationships are a mirror image for the pathway of self-awareness. True peace must be discovered in your own being before it can be shared. Frequently your journey may seem lonely, but it is your own Truth that must be found first. There will, however, be many guidelines indicating the direction of your life; all must be used. Sadness and celebration will alternate until, in the light of awareness, duality will disappear. Life is not a static phenomenon and earthly time can never be transcended simply because it has no reality. Many blessings, in warmth we touch and in light you will be guided.

November 24, 1991 - Angela

When you share your love with others it multiplies to fill your being with warmth and tenderness. To care for another is to care for the One. All are expressions of the totality of the Oneness. Love can be found everywhere. In sadness it is the warmth of the teardrop upon the cheek and in laughter it is the ripple of laughter's music within the heart. When you touch another in tenderness, remember, your hand becomes the loving hand of the One. There is no other way love can be expressed, save by the movement of life's energy through each being. Remember love wherever you may be. Look for it in the eyes of the child and the faces of those who may seek your guidance and help. Remember also, that only a perfect channel is able to transmit the full power of the healing energy of love. Continue in your own way to cleanse and filter the impurities and illusions from your life, help will be given. The deepest desire is to express and to receive love; the ways for this expression must always be kept open. We link with you in love, please open the fullness of your heart to receive life's blessings.

The droplet does not seek the ocean nor the fish the sea until it flounders helplessly upon the beach.

The sound of many hands applauding earthly achievements does not add one cubit to spiritual growth.

Yesterday's regrets and tomorrow's ambitions zealously guard the temple of the mystical moment.

November 30, 1991 - Claire

Love is the poetry of life. A poetry not of words but an energy bursting forth from the heart. It is not possible to understand love, it is beyond understanding and has no roots in the human mind. Male and female aspects of the One are expressed bringing the deepest fulfillment to the open heart. Woman has the potential to love completely. Man can only love partially; it is not in his nature to totally surrender to the power of love, his life has other aspects to express. When you give your love, asking for no reward, you are attuned to the chords of light. Expect no acclaim and remember also that a heart opening totally is vulnerable. That is the very nature of love, there can be no other way. Share the spiritual gifts of the heart fearlessly, remembering that the qualities of love's warmth and tenderness require naught save their own expression. Sing the poetry of love and let your dreams tell only of the palaces of light

and the rainbow's bridge.   In your dreams you will discover a reality
and the bridge will become your link with those who will guide you
on your way.

December 1991 - Tricia

Search in your heart and you will find all that is true.   Searching
in the mind to solve life's problems may only bring distress.   An un-
awakened mind often produces manifestations that fake the illusion
of reality, a virtual reality.   It is mind that fabricates the paths and
the apparent cross-roads on life's journey.   There are no illusions in
the heart, though it frequently becomes difficult to seek its guidance.
Heart will align with your true destiny, while mind aligns with your
fears, seeing your destiny as fate and frequently actually creating
the situations you are most afraid of.   However, when wisdom and
awareness are applied to the deeper aspects of life, we know that
there is no chooser of reality.   Reality appears in its own light, not
presenting problems only facts.

There are many aspects of meditation and it is frequently used
as a panacea to quell the disturbance of an insatiable mind.   True
meditation is seeing the panorama of reality as it unfolds its mul-
titudinous colours woven by the spirit as it seeks the light.   The
carpet you weave on the loom of the heart will present a spectacle
beyond your wildest dreams as you view it in retrospect after your
realization of Truth, Love and Light.

*Laughter has the same quality as the summer breeze, arising magically
from an unknown source, it plays joyfully with those who would listen to
its music.*

*The tiny seed and the mighty oak rooted in the earth share the same
desire for the light. Can you not discover the very same longing in your
own heart?*

Question: *When will I awaken to Love?*

The night has its purpose - for spirit must rest awhile, regaining energy to greet the dawn. When the glory of the morning light appears, dreams of the slumbering hours will be left far behind. The cyclical nature of life provides restful periods for spirit, both in sleep and death. When you awaken to the light of love it will be the clarion call of the heart beckoning you to meet the ever renewing quality of life as it presents itself to the heart that is open. No poetic words of the bard can ever tell of a loving heart. It must be experienced by spirit in its own way. Remember also, it is a heavy heart crying out for love filled to the brim with broken dreams that eventually breaks open to receive the true gifts of love. The false values of yesterday must be discarded when you awaken, allowing true love to play her melody in your heart. When you awaken you will perceive the past only as a companion who traveled with you for a while bringing you towards the dawn of ultimate Truth. Many blessings.

December 10, 1991 - Sheila

Love can never be known, it can only be lived through the creative vibrations of a heart seeking alignment with the deeper values of life. Love is a delicate flower that can never be known, though many may, in their ignorance, endeavor to dissect and destroy its beauty. To know the blossom, stem, root, and seed would reveal the nature of our universe. Perceive how flower's root draws sustenance from the earth while still paying homage to the light. Surely the origin of the seed will forever remain a divine mystery. But see flower casts her seeds forth so they may propagate her beauty into the timeless future. It is in the wonder of the blossom that love resides, displaying her glory to enhance the bouquet of love. In flower's blossom, light is miraculously transformed into Nature's love song, expressing a perfect harmony between heaven and earth.

Can you not cultivate the same relationship in your own life? For surely, it is the very same law that binds each atom in our universe. In awareness of the divine trinity of heaven, earth, and the creative energy of love, life can produce the most exquisite blossoms, the true embodiment of the power of love, showering its blessing on all who share our garden. Flower's seed may find its own fertile land often far away from the cradle of its birth. The secrets of Nature's love can never be known; they can only be lived and experienced by an open heart. As the flower head turns its face to the light to discover its blessing, it is also necessary for spirits to lift their heads towards the light, not in an endeavor to discover the unknowable mystery, but in the deepest homage to the eternal power of love and light.

The persistent visitor knocking at the door of your heart is love, she will never go away until you welcome her in.

December 1, 1991 - Lydia

Love is the greatest mystery and we seek many answers to the insoluble. There can be no formula to discover the very core of life. Love is that core, it can only be experienced, never understood. In the moments of silence, love will come, the spaces between each heartbeat are the fertile soil for the growth of love. Look not to fill those spaces in your life, they are very meaningful, the nursery of life's energy. The most delicate flower cannot flourish in a tangled undergrowth, the way must be prepared for the seed to grow. When you are silent and your heart is still, much can be given. Use your moments of silence to bring forth love's blossom in your heart as your desire for happiness is surrendered. The fleeting butterfly of happiness will soon disappear into the evening mist. There will be the greater gifts of joy and bliss to be bestowed upon you as your inner space is cultivated. Love will blossom in a most wondrous way. It will be more beautiful than your wildest dreams, as your heart opens to Truth, your soil will radiate with love's ever renewing light.

December 3, 1991 - Laura

To understand the phases of life is to live in harmony with nature. There are many peaks and many troughs, many mountains and many valleys. When sun sinks low in the evening sky and the storm seems imminent, rest for a while in the shelter of the valley; surely the peace of the valley will shield you from the violent storm. It can never be possible to live forever at the summit. Many storms will come and often you may find protection necessary until you become stronger. When storm subsides at the dawning of a new day, you may lift your head towards the sky to view your peak. Till then rest in your valley, giving thanks to all who have shown the way. In moments of stillness, feel the loving touch of Mother Nature's hand caressing her child. Enjoy the beauty of the valley. See how magnificent are the colourful flowers, listen silently to the music of the trees, and hear Nature's silver voice singing in the babbling brook. All that is required is a deep acceptance, trusting in all that calls your heart. Has not heart been your guide transporting you so lovingly into the restful peace of the valley? If your mind becomes disturbed perhaps it has not understood the message of the valley. Mind can seldom know valley's peace, but you are not your mind, you are much more. Learn to watch mind's turbulence, as it beckons you away from your heart. When the dawn of a new day appears, commence your ascent to find your temple upon the mountain top. In the meanwhile, let the valley recharge your spirit with its energy. Many blessings as you rest in beauty.

Perceive how swiftly ripened fruit falls towards the earth. The law of gravity is so well demonstrated here, but I beseech thee to remember the perfect law of grace that raised fruit's seed from the rich soil towards the sky.

January 1, 1993 - Life's Magical Playhouse

There are many entrances and many exits in the stage play of life, but always remember you can watch from the auditorium. But perhaps there may be occasions when you must leave your seat and move onto the stage with other participants in life's drama, but deep down you know it is not real, just a stage play written by your mind. There will be entrances to be welcomed and others to view with disdain as you identify with each character upon the platform. It is natural there may be many who you regard as unworthy of the role they may be playing, others will be commended by your mind for their dramatic abilities. Give your love and thanks to players who will be leaving your theater, they have enacted their part well. Show great appreciation for their performance, but always remember it is most necessary to provide space upon your platform for new players to enact their roles. Others will inevitably receive your invitation to attend and take their place upon life's stage. Welcome them with enthusiasm, they have learnt and rehearsed their parts for countless incarnations, soon they will appear as the curtain of the next act rises in your life. Remember, you may join the performance at any time you wish, but it is more important to remind yourself that you have a seat in the auditorium that you can return to at any moment. The new players upon your stage may need guidance in the roles they are portraying and it is here that you can be of great assistance. Yes, this is the stage play of life! Have you not observed the many entrances and many exits of past performances? You may laugh at the comedy, marvel at the love story, applaud the courage of the hero and dance with the beautiful ballerina; but pray, do not condemn the villain or fret over the tragedy, remember, it is you who have written the script with your own mind. Enjoy each interval, each act, each scene, and every player.

December 9, 1992 - Nick

Hunger pains of the physical body can be easily experienced as the stomach is denied an intake of food - this desire must be satiated - enabling earthly life to continue. We now speak of another more subtle hunger; subtle, yet of paramount importance. This hunger is that of the soul, requiring nutriment for growth. Pain, fear, unhappiness are but the hunger pains of your soul crying out for the love, so long denied. Listen carefully to the voices that call asking for your recognition. Yes, you have experienced much pain in your life, but how else could your heart communicate the hunger of the soul. Now is the feeding time though it must start slowly, for your heart could not contain a sudden intake of great sustenance. Your fear and pain, remember, are not only voices crying out in your wilderness, they are also vehicles in which you can travel towards true fulfill-ment. Life is now at an acute turning point for many who seek the light. Trust deeply in the signs at the crossroads of your life, but pray, do not linger by the signposts for too long.

January 12, 1993 - Stephen

Love may be expressed as a wave of the very highest vibration. The speed of love's energy enables it to manifest everywhere, not governed by the confines of an imaginary time or space. There can be no part of our vast boundless universe devoid of love. If you feel you may have lost love's blessing, I say in truth - this is but an illusion of your mind. In awareness, love can be discovered everywhere. You may not be able to perceive love by sensory imput, but always remember it is never absent. Perhaps you have sought contentment and happiness through the limited perception of ego-mind, but please know deeply, this is an energy manifesting at a much lower frequency. At this level mind can discover and identify with coarser vibrations. This, however, can never bring true fulfillment to your heart. The nature of mind requires a constant longing for the unattainable.

Mind can no more discover love than it can find the magic essence of the rose when the search seems to be of a far greater importance.

You may well ask how to experience the high frequencies of love, but remember, all questions are born from mind, ego-mind can never comprehend or attune to the highest levels of existence. You may retune to higher frequencies in the space of your silent moments. In this space you can discover the true nature of your being. When this quality manifests, there will be others attracted by the new dimension of light that you have found. Life must work in many mysterious ways and it can not be possible for your mind to understand events which appear to have no meaning, perhaps leaving you feeling frustrated and helpless. But, ironically, it is only in this state, when mind surrenders its search, the essence of love can be found pulsating within your own heart.

January 17, 1993 - Simon

Energy attracts like. In awareness you will know you possess the inherent ability to retune your being to many varied frequencies of energy. All is available. Often you may have denied the manifestation of emotional energy. Perhaps you sought to control your emotions because they seemed to cause much disturbance in your life. In Truth this disturbance is of the utmost importance. In the turbulence of emotion there are many possibilities, as the reality of life is presented. Emotion is movement; is there any part of our universe not in a constant state of flux?

When you accept and align with emotional energy you align with the atomic power of the galaxies. To suppress emotion is akin to destroying a part of your being. Each relationship in life, remember, is a reflection of an inner dimension in yourself, possibly a dimension that you have not accepted, in this context it becomes most necessary to understand the nature of the relationship, so your own knowing becomes deeper. The deeper you move into life, the deeper you move into yourself. Perhaps this may not be the direction in which you desired to travel, but it is the only worthwhile journey. You may try to deny emotional clouds appearing on the horizon, but why not use the energy of the storm to take you deeper within to discover your truth?

February 6, 1993

To trust in the wisdom of life may become very arduous when you are apparently faced with seemingly impossible difficulties and the pain becomes too intense to bear. But when you look back on your life you will find that your life has been blessed with much love, although it may not have been in the way you expected it. It is true also, there were many tears to fill your heart. In truth these tears were the raindrops of love sent to nurture the fragile seeds in your garden. Without the blessings of both love and tears, each life appears meaningless, but you have received the raindrops bravely. Now is the time to open wide the doorway of your heart to allow even greater energy of love to fill your being with the healing rays of light. There is naught to fear but fear itself, and you will find in truth, that your fears seldom live up to your expectations!

Life has many masquerades and you must peer through the veil of illusion that creates your anxiety. When the phenomenon of life and death are perceived clearly all fears will fade in the knowing that there is no death, **only the denial of life**. Universal energy is constantly reforming; at each moment your new life can commence when the past attitudes of your mind change. This is life's greatest discovery, the knowing that inner awareness of truth can change the outer aspects of your being. Attitude is the powerful weapon you can wield at any moment you may choose, to cut away the residual pain of the past and unrealistic fears for the future. Trust in the infinite wisdom of life - there can be no greater guide and no brighter light to guide you safely through the darkness. Look now, can you not see our light and feel the energy of our love as we touch?

December 15, 1992 - Marion

Each moment can become an opportunity for self discovery. Although outside pressures of life many seem intent upon leading you away from your center, know in your heart that although there man be much activity at the circumference of life's wheel the hub always remains still. In the fiercest tempest or the raging storm, the central focal point remains calm. The life you have chosen will inevitably create much activity. Enjoy the thrill of movement, remembering the analogy of the wheel. Often when faced with frustrating and seemingly impossible circumstances, it may seem impossible to discover a meaning for events apparently causing much frustration, but in awareness, this feeling can be used to transport you to your still center. Earthly life, remember, is a series of farewells and also of meetings. Often you must bid farewell to all that is illusory so a meeting with Truth becomes possible. Truth, Reality, the True Self, Trust, and Faith are most valuable qualities though they may seem very difficult to acquire when others do not meet up to your expectations. When I speak of trust it is in its truest sense, a deep trust in life and all that is presented. Change is an inevitable process. As you look back upon your life you may well discover that frequently the darkest curses turn into the most valuable golden blessings.

February 10, 1993 - Liz

In the tranquillity of silence much becomes possible, in silence a deep connection is formed with the inner being, the true self you have forgotten as you slumber deeply in the world of dreams. In the sacred space of silence, the creative side of your real nature is able to express the deepest feelings of the heart and dispel the illusions of darkness seemingly besetting your life. Although at times you may appear to live in darkness, know truly that it is but a dark veil woven by treads of fear. In truth, there is no darkness, for even in the darkest night sky you will find your star shining ever brighter. All that is required is for you to open your eyes to the light existing everywhere. Loneliness too is a great illusion, only ego-mind creates separation. In truth you will know that all is inextricably joined by divine creative energy, an energy that you may term "love", linking each wave, each particle and each soul in our universe. Remember always, in your silent moods there is a strong connection with the creative energy you may choose to call, God, the name matters not.

To touch the world with beauty is but an expression of universal love. To touch the world with beauty is to show love's true wonder to many hearts, but always remember your spirit within, for that spirit too must share the gifts of love. Listen constantly to your heart in moments of silence and you will surely discover beauty and truth in your life as the veils of darkness and fear are dissolved by the light you find within. Live each beautiful moment fully and it is truly blessed.

February 1993 - Paula

You have a magic lamp to enlighten your life. Although this lamp shines from deep in your being it also has the power to illuminate your outer world. Subconscious mind has been your faithful servant obeying your commands *without discrimination*. Pray look around and you will undoubtedly see that nothing appearing in your outer world has not existed as a thought. Choose your thoughts with deep awareness, but remember, your wish must be realistic and *for you alone*. You may request anything you desire, but not everything.

Your choice will inevitably appear in your world, but a word of caution here, your wish may not be granted in the way that you expected. Without inner illumination there can be much frustration as you battle with circumstances presenting many problems in your life, but look deeply within, you will find that your wish has been granted albeit in a strange way.   You may have heard that new lamps can be exchanged for old, that is only an illusion.   Your lamp has always been present, emanating from the same power source, no new lamp could ever replace it.   Perhaps you feel your magic lamp has become dull and has lost its luster. Pray remember, all that is valuable must be tended with great care, your inner light is no exception.   Polish it with the alchemy of love and you will find the luster still there beneath the surface.   When your inner light burns brightly it will enlighten every aspect of your life and those sharing your outer world.   Do not waste energy endeavoring to change the outer world.   Look within, polish your lamp of inner love and perceive its radiance illuminating the world you have created from your thoughts. It is then you will find many conditions changing in your life - there can be no other way to your Truth.

February 11, 1993 - On Healing

The greatest events are born from the smallest beginning, as the most devastating forest fire can spring from a tiny spark. The fire of love also often remains dormant in many hearts, but in wisdom you may know that you can use your love to ignite the spark in others.   Surely when the flame burns brighter it will spread into many hearts and propagate its own energy into a darkened world.

When confronted by pain, poverty, and distress in your world, there seems at first naught we can do to create a better quality of life for the sufferer - it is true - love is within each spirit, but that love lies dormant frequently masked by the cloak of darkness and fear. The very first requirement must therefore be to **polish the mirror of your own light** enabling it to shine more brightly.   Can you not see that the brightest light shines over greater distances.   Yes, our own source of love is the magic potion to alleviate much pain and distress.   Many believe it is absolutely necessary to move nearer to the darkness of the suffering spirit, in their minds this may well be true. However, in your own corner of the world it becomes possible to touch others far away, to touch them with the wonder of your own inner light as it shines into their world. Remember, though, it can only be reflected by your own mirror of pure consciousness. This you may well discover is your contribution to remove darkness from others. Dream not of distant lands or traveling to the four corners of the earth to help others, life is throbbing now within you. This is the time, this is also the place, so it will always be. In the beginning you may not be aware of your ability to spread and also beam the energy of light, as you become more aware, however, your life's purpose will be revealed. Wait patiently and trust in a greater wisdom; patience is one of the greatest spiritual qualities. From trust and wisdom, light propagates from your heart as recognition of your life's true purpose.

When you share your love with others it multiplies, filling your being with warmth and tenderness. To care for another is to care for the One; for is not each soul a facet and a unique expression of the totality of oneness? Love can be found everywhere, in sadness it is the warmth of a teardrop upon a cheek, and is not joy the singing stream of laughter in your heart? When you touch another in tenderness, know that your hand becomes the loving hand of the One. There can be no greater medium for love's expression than warmth and tenderness. Love exists in all things and in all people, but it is our knowing and willingness to share its light that will propagate its seeds into a barren world unaware of its blessing. Can there be a more worthwhile purpose for your life?

If you climb high enough,
the biggest problems become much smaller
when your viewpoint changes.

Remember love wherever you may be, in joy and also in the sadness of teardrops of those who may seek your compassion.

Know that the warmth in your heart is the perfect channel for transmission of love's healing energy. **Touch only with love, so those you touch may be warmed by the glow of you tenderness**. Life's deepest desire is to express and receive love. Pathways for this expression and reception must always remain open and available if the healing channel is to remain effective; continue in your own way to cleanse your channel, filtering impurities, fear, and illusions from your life. Links are formed with you in love and truth when you open the fullness of your heart to the tender light of the One.

In cathedrals and churches, stained glass has no luster until viewed from within. Inner light also enhances the beauty of earthly love. The glittering gem of life has many brilliant unseen facets vibrating with colour when light shines upon them. Perceive how earthly diamonds can also reflect the glory of the sky.

December 8, 1992 - Peter

Perhaps you have slept within the darkness of mind's fears for too long. Can you not now feel in your heart that your long night is ending? Remember, a seed sown into the earth may experience much pain as the husk is opened. But no life can be fulfilled, no growth possible, until that seed emerges from the dark earth to find the light. When the darkness is at its deepest, remember, dawn is near. It becomes most necessary for you to awaken slowly for the pain of the past has retained a strong hold upon your mind. In your heart you know, you are not your mind, your thoughts or your fears. You are an expression of creativity that is much greater, much deeper and of a far greater quality. Now the time to trust has arrived. The seed can do naught but trust as it opens to the light and this will now become your direction. Lift your gaze away from the caverns and as you emerge, perceive the golden light of your new day dawning upon the horizon. To trust in the new light may at first seem to present some difficulty as your eyes have been closed for so long. You also may find those in your life who would attempt to destroy that trust. Pay small heed, for they may still continue to live in the darkness you have left, remember the past only with gratitude. Surely it was the darkness of the caverns in which you lived for so long that forced you to discover the very pathway towards the light you are beginning to see. Look deeply within your heart, there you will discover the love, light, and the wisdom enabling you to scribe the coming chapters of your life's book.

Sun must rise to its zenith to break the tenuous hold of the morning dewdrop upon the rose.
But naught can dim the sparkling glory of its luster for it seeks not to cling to that which will surely be taken away.

Perhaps you may remember the words of a great teacher who once walked upon your earth plane. Although his footsteps remain but imprints in the sands of time, his love remains. For in his love you were bidden to cast off those parts of the body which offended you. The words have never really been understood and it would do well to meditate upon them. The references were, in truth, to the ballast of the astral body, the desire body, for herein lies the un-awakened consciousness, the ignorance of man, locked in the darkness of his earthly desires. The physical body acquired genetically by heredity and transmission, eventually becomes the astral body, bringing unfulfilled desires or so-called "karma" from past dreams into another life. Why not cast away the ballast of past conditioning and ascend to the greatest heights of awakened consciousness in a new awareness of the light? There is no debt to pay to the past of an awakened one!

April 23, 1990

In temples, mosques and churches you may discover beauty. However, it is a beauty that does not carry the life seed. Life's mysterious magical seed is found only in that which lives or breathes. You will undoubtedly discover great artistry and creation in your places of worship but seldom creativity. Creation belongs to the past. Creativity is forever present in the eternal now; a living seed pulsating with the very essence of the universe. Oft times we have spoken of Nature's creativity; an ever reminding message of life's meaning. The breath of the wind and the flower's upturned head towards the sky can be far worthier teachers than those often found in the most glorious temples of worship. Looking down to worship footprints of another's path in the sand may make you miss your own way. Lift your gaze to the sky and let the flowers, the trees, the lakes, and creatures of the earth, sea, and air become your gurus and follow them to the light!

There are many candles burning in your temples, though I tell you in truth, to light the joy of life in another's eyes will exceed the total brilliance of all earth's holy candles burning together.

Your tomorrow is an embryo growing in the womb of today, gathering all the sustenance of conscious need, so it may awaken in wonder to the light.

The child of tomorrow is surely fed by the thoughts of this day.

Would you seek anything but love for the child of the morrow?

In the acorn exists the mighty oak and in your heart the plan implanted to become a shining star.

All pathways lead towards the light. In the beginning, it is the light of understanding that dawns upon the horizon of human consciousness; understanding can be conveyed by words and symbols. This first dawn eventually becomes lost in the brilliance of the day as sun rises towards her zenith. Understanding is then transformed into the stem of knowing. Trust is the leaf upon that stem and love-light the ultimate blossom.

May 2, 1995 Selma - Florida

Life gives and life also takes away, that is the nature of the perfect law, there can be no other way. However, each earthly life is presented as an opportunity to discover the gift that will remain yours forever. This gift awaiting your reclamation is the unchanging essence of your true reality. Look within at this and every moment you will surely discover the same witness who perceived movements and growth through various phases of your life. This unchanging presence is your very nature, traveling with you on many journeys through time. Perhaps when immersed in the pain and the turmoil of your everyday world it seems difficult to discover this elemental essence. Know in your heart though, soul's presence resides in realms unaffected by apparent changes in the physical world. You may frequently question the purpose of a life seemingly to be just a brief interlude in the scenario of time; in truth though, your earthly quest is to find your own reality and to celebrate the discovery of this eternal treasure in your own heart.

May 3, 1995 - Rachel

The world in which you live is woven into a pattern by your dreams. Many may believe that each one shares the same world. But this is just not true. You are the creator of the world in which you appear to live. On your journeys through the hallways of time you have acquired many wonderful gifts. Weave them wisely with the threads of creative imagination to make your world vibrant with creations' colours. You may have heard that eyes are the windows of your soul, but without the inner beauty of your reality, no light could shine on the outer world of your dreams. Beauty may be in the eye of the beholder and you will surely discover it as love shining eternally from your heart center. Love is the very creative process of life itself, pulsating as a wave in every cell of your being and also in every atomic particle of our vast universe. Always remember the magical power of the imagination; the creative process within. Use it to paint your pictures on the canvas of your life; the scenario of your outer world. Know that although you are a unique creator of your world, it still becomes possible to share a common dream with another. Weave your dreams with love and they will surely be of the utmost splendour, even when somber colours appear on the backdrop of your life.

Battle not with the somber shadows, the warriors of light are surrounding the fortress of your fears, surrender your illusions for their defeat is inevitable.

February 20, 1997 - Sue

Would you deny the beauty of the magical rose in the deepest night? Although its beauty remains unseen, the memory of its magical essence remains as love in your heart forever. Eyes have been given so you may see the beauty of your outer world, but when you look deeply within, in your silent moments, another vast realm of a far greater reality is revealed. Inability or unwillingness to become aware of its presence does not signify its nonexistence, for it will forever remain a presence awaiting your acknowledgement. When your world is viewed only through the limited perception of sensory input, the totality and the beauty of all life cannot be perceived. What mind could conceive the dawn without the sunset and equally without unawareness of beauty, how could beauty's eternal reality be demonstrated when dawn arises to dispel the darkness? Surely then the beauty of the rose is seen again with earthly eyes. On pathways to Truth, it may often become necessary for outer worlds created by mind's sensors, to be interrupted or even disrupted, before inner eyes can be opened revealing life in a new light. When the light of your new dawn arises, pray cast your gaze away from the long shadow of the rose upon the earth to behold rose's full glory blossoming eternally as love within your heart. Many Blessings on your journey to the light.

Light cannot cohabit with darkness, neither can fear and love share the same dwelling.
Fear forever remains a formidable barrier to those who would venture towards the threshold of their heart.

Pray measure not the light years to your distant star whilst it patiently awaits your discovery in your own heart.

The alchemy of love changes life's obstacles into stepping stones on your pathway to Truth.

Perceive how the teardrops from dark clouds blend with light etching a most glorious rainbow on your inner sky.

I speak of environment...each organism requires conditions conducive to its growth. Without the correct environment - seed will rot, decay and return to the soil, to provide sustenance for other life forms. Become aware that you also may consciously or unconsciously choose the location for your earthly existence. Flower's resplendent beauty is a glorious tribute to the soil that nurtured its growth and fulfillment, providing the correct environment for its ultimate blossom. Surely the blossom expresses its thanks to the bough and the bough to the tree trunk that bears its weight. The trunk also in gratitude spreads her twisting roots into the fertile soil in deep thanksgiving for the decay that made life possible. Can you not perceive a perfect harmony on all levels? The fragrant beauty of the lotus may have been conceived in mud, yet this was the correct environment for its growth. In human life too, your growth is made possible by a combination of many elements and energy, combining in love in the correct environment to nurture your life form. Would you withhold your gratitude from the Sun, the Earth, and the ever flowing river as you grow towards the light?

Observe the quality of the polished mirror, grasping nothing, refusing nothing, retaining naught save the brightness of its own nature.

Hard rocks must eventually surrender to the soft water when their structure dissolves into the sands of time.

Nature's Frontiers

All is one, yet there are many tangible divisions between the organic and in-organic realms. Perceive clearly the dividing lines, Nature draws to separate her kingdoms. Awareness of this ever perfect law may enable you to penetrate a deeper level of reality. What stone could ever know the splendour of the tree stretching her limbs towards the sky, or could the tree imagine the tender maternity of the bird nesting in the protective foliage of her leaves? The animal world, although organic, can never know the joy and sadness to be found in a human heart. Nature in her infinite wisdom only reveals her secrets to those who are ready to receive them. What mind could turn the stone into a tree, the tree into a singing bird, or allow the bird to cross the protective barrier from the animal kingdom into the heart of man? Her frontiers are guarded most zealously awaiting your readiness and your call. It is only this call that can dissolve the barriers of Nature's kingdoms. The call from your heart will be heard and you will be able to cross the frontier into souls' Kingdom of Light, you may term the fourth dimension.

Is it a dream?

Would your dreams conjure up illusions deep of perfect love and light, a utopian land, no pain no death, no darkness for the light to rest? But who in life's journey has traveled far, perhaps it was a dream and where were those arms so warm with love to comfort when no pain was felt? What cruel blow did fate cast upon our head to weave pains illusion into our veil of dreams so sweet? Or would the fearsome devil torture souls in his darkest dungeon deep? Yet no blame condemns, in truth it was a phantom of the mind, no blow smitten by hand of fate but passions longing, desire, fear and ignorance, these are the culprits who turn the screws on life's torturous rack of pain.

This meditation was given in 1991 during breakfast at a Paris hotel.
Originally written on a serviette:

The Temple Meditation

Come, I will guide you towards a temple of indescribable wonder standing on yonder horizon, but there is no journey to be made, for the sanctuary of which I speak lies in the depths of your own being. Pause awhile, look within, a light shines brightly from the tower, beckoning towards temple's inner chambers, beyond the portals. Can you not now see a golden spire reaching high into the sky? There is no bell to chime any hours of earthly time, or sound to summon worshipers to temple's gateway, but the light in the tower is a beacon guiding us towards an entrance. Move nearer, observe firm columns supporting its structure, admire the wonderful carvings on temple's outer walls, created by many loving hands, working through countless lifetimes.   See... now the door is there before us, great and sturdy in its structure, protecting many price-less treasures within temple's chambers.

I cannot accompany you upon your inner journey, now I must bid thee farewell as we reach the threshold, but before I go I will tell of many secrets and wonders you will find within: Firstly you must visit the dark crypt, here lie achievements, hopes, desires, and regrets, born through the span of many earthly incarnations, but see, they are cloaked in the shroud of death. As you decend into dark dank chambers , there will be many fears to face, as ghosts of the past appear before you. Be not afraid though, remember the light you carry within can dispel the fears of the past and guide you safely through the darkness. As you increase the light from your magical lantern, each specter will disappear; they were mere illusions created by shadows of your mind.

Enough of the darkness, now you must climb the stairway to discover temple's full glory, as you ascend you will hear soft sweet music, enhanced by golden voices chanting within, though I tell you in truth, no earthly choir has ever sung their hymns here. Go more deeply, you will begin to see a golden light shining from a half open doorway, you may open it wide to perceive the fullest glory of your temple. Enter silently to perceive a wondrous light of the greatest intensity, emanating from the altar, immersing your whole being in love, you will be dazed by its radiance. You will find no prayer books or religious symbols upon the altar or figures of an unknown icon or illusory deity to worship, only temple's inner light.

Gaze through the eastern window to behold the magnificence of the sunrise. As dawn bestows her gift upon your temple, each translucent colour, each facet will come alive with hues far more resplendent than the most glorious rainbow born from earth and sky, vibrating with the very essence of our universe. Wait awhile, as earthly day passes, perceive through your western window, the full glory of sunset, painting each column with glittering gold, a gold far more precious than even the purest metal mined from earth. Look intensely at the fabric of your temple, you will see only light supporting the edifice. Pause for a moment to marvel at its glory, knowing deeply in your heart that you are the architect and builder of your temple.

But see, there is another chamber beckoning from a deeper recess within. Here you must enter with great reverence, this chamber is the inner sanctum of your soul, in this sacred silent space, you will discover a flame burning brightly, not fed by any fossilized fuel, but eternally kindled by the energy of the love and light of each star in our boundless universe. Meditate upon the inner flame and you will disappear. This is the greatest secret of your innermost chamber... you are that flame. Although the outer walls of your temple dwelling will be eroded by passage of earthly time, I say in truth, your inner flame can never be extinguished; neither the terrestrial tempest, nor earth's most fearsome flood, can quench soul's flame; know this when you return once more into the energy of your outer physical world. Do not seek me upon the steps as you leave, for I must return to the crossroads to guide other travelers towards their unique inner journey. When you depart you will carry soul's gift with you, an immense blessing, you may take and share with many wherever you may go... never doubt its presense. Look into life's swiftly flowing river, you will see soul's light reflected clearly within its water. Look also into the silent lakes in the eyes of those around you, here too you will see a reflection of your own inner flame. There can be no greater blessing bestowed upon you, this flame is the gift of love...look around and within, you can discover it everywhere.

Thank you for your words.

Response: Love requires naught for it surely exalts in its own fulfillment. I take your thoughts though as a greeting and an acknowledgement of the eternal link we have forged with our family...
     In my greeting to you, I send the purity of the morning light and the wonder of the flower's reflected glory, the harmony of Nature's sounds within her trees, the soft summer breeze, and the sound of the songbird soaring to unknown heights. When you hear these sounds, lift your head towards your star, feel my love as I draw closer to you. Know also that I am there, not only in your silent moments, but also in the activity of your outer world - although you may have forgotten me, I have not forgotten you.

Meditate on the love within and surrounding you, there is no greater way to express your gratitude.

Many Blessings,
Omano

The contents of this book are extracts from inspired personal writings given to many over the last ten years. They have proved to be of a great help and comfort to those seeking a deeper meaning to their lives.

The writings are often carried each day continuing to give guidance and love from the Omano energy.

If you would like to receive your own heartfelt words please contact Gillian at:

The Omano Center
33 Sea Place, Goring by Sea
West Sussex BN12 4 BZ UK

Telephone: 01903 246240 (from Europe)
                      011-44-1903-246240 (from USA)

Fax: 01903 247145 - for further details
E-Mail omano-centre@fastnet.co.uk

About the Author

Jack Joseph was born in London in 1925, trained as a communication engineer and served as a radar technician with the Royal Air Force. He became a yoga teacher in 1974. Married with five children, living now in Sussex U.K., Jack commenced writing in 1987 with the first Omano words. He has travelled extensively throughout the world with his wife Gillian, sharing the words, wisdom and love of Omano with many souls who were mysteriously drawn into their energy field. The writings, have and continue to be, a source of great comfort and guidance to those seeking a deeper meaning to their lives.